KT-382-438

ESSENTIAL
Fish &
Seafood

p

Contents

Introduction

Presently there are more than 30,000 different species of fish from all over the world, ranging in shape, size and colour. It is easy to purchase any kind of fish nowadays, whether it be some herring common around the British shores, or the bright blue parrot fish of the Seychelles.

Fish can be divided into three main categories. Round sea fish is the largest group and includes fish such as cod, mackerel and red mullet. These fish can be tiny like whitebait or huge like sharks. Such fish are usually sold whole, in fillets or in cutlets (steaks).

Sole, halibut and plaice are among the fish included in the flat sea fish category. These fish swim on their sides and are easy to identify because of their distinctive colouring (dark on one side and white on the other) and the unusual positioning of both eyes on the same side of the head. With the exception of turbot, halibut and skate flat fish are usually sold whole or filleted.

The last group is freshwater fish which includes fish such as pike and salmon. All of these fish are born in rivers or lakes, however some of

them, such as salmon, spend all of their adult lives in the ocean only returning to the river of their birth to spawn. These fish are becoming easier to purchase, especially as many supermarkets now have fresh seafood counters.

When buying fish ensure that it is absolutely fresh. Recognising fresh fish is easy as its natural skin colour should still be apparent. Also, check the appearance of the fish's eyes. If they look white, sunken or dry the fish is old and should not be purchased. Other signs of freshness are red gills, a firm body, tightly fitted scales and a pleasant smell.

Fish is extremely good for you as it has a low fat content and contains many vitamins and nutrients such as iron, B vitamins, calcium, fluorine and sometimes calcium. It also cooks very quickly, therefore is an excellent food for those in a hurry. When cooking fish be careful not to overcook it as it will become tough and dry. Instead cook lightly until tender. Cooking fish is similar to cooking

an egg, just cook until the proteins begin to set. It is even more important when eating raw fish to be sure that it is completely fresh, and like all fish it should be eaten on the day of purchase.

Shell fish such as shrimps, lobster and mussels are a great alternative and are equally as nutritious and delicious. However, once again shell fish deteriorate very quickly and should be bought for immediate consumption only.

Mussel & Potato Soup

Serves 4

INGREDIENTS

750 g/1 lb 10 oz mussels
2 tbsp olive oil
100 g/3¹/₂ oz/7 tbsp unsalted
    butter
2 slices rindless, fatty bacon,
    chopped
1 onion, chopped
2 garlic cloves, crushed

60 g/2 oz/¹/₂ cup plain
    (all purpose) flour
450 g/1 lb potatoes, thinly
    sliced
100 g/3¹/₂ oz/³/₄ cup
    dried conchigliette
300 ml/¹/₂ pint/1¹/₄ cups
    double (heavy) cream

1 tbsp lemon juice
2 egg yolks
salt and pepper

TO GARNISH:
2 tbsp finely chopped fresh
    parsley
lemon wedges

1 Debeard the mussels and scrub them under cold water for 5 minutes. Discard any mussels that do not close immediately when sharply tapped.

2 Bring a large pan of water to the boil, add the mussels, oil and a little pepper and cook until the mussels open.

3 Drain the mussels, reserving the cooking liquid. Discard any mussels

that are closed. Remove the mussels from their shells.

4 Melt the butter in a large saucepan and cook the bacon, onion and garlic for 4 minutes. Stir in the flour, then 1.2 litres/ 2 pints/5 cups of the reserved cooking liquid.

5 Add the potatoes to the pan and simmer for 5 minutes. Add the conchigliette and simmer for a further 10 minutes.

6 Add the cream and lemon juice, season to taste, then add the mussels to the pan.

7 Blend the egg yolks with 1-2 tbsp of the remaining cooking liquid, stir into the pan and cook for 4 minutes.

8 Ladle the soup into 4 warm individual soup bowls, garnish with the chopped fresh parsley and lemon wedges and serve.

Italian Fish Soup

Serves 4

INGREDIENTS

60 g/2 oz/4 tbsp butter
450 g/1 lb assorted fish fillets, such as red mullet and snapper
450 g/1 lb prepared seafood, such as squid and prawns (shrimp)
225 g/8 oz fresh crabmeat
1 large onion, sliced

25 g/1 oz/^{1}/4 cup plain (all purpose) flour
1.2 litres/2 pints/5 cups fish stock
100 g/3^1/2 oz/^{3}/4 cup dried pasta shapes, such as ditalini or elbow macaroni
1 tbsp anchovy essence

grated rind and juice of 1 orange
50 ml/2 fl oz/^{1}/2 cup dry sherry
300 ml/^{1}/2 pint/1^1/4 cups double (heavy) cream
salt and black pepper
crusty brown bread, to serve

1 Melt the butter in a large saucepan and cook the fish fillets, seafood, crabmeat and onion over a low heat for 6 minutes.

2 Stir the flour into the mixture.

3 Gradually add the fish stock and bring to the boil, stirring constantly. Reduce the heat and simmer for 30 minutes.

4 Add the pasta and cook for 10 minutes.

5 Stir in the anchovy essence, orange rind, orange juice, sherry and double (heavy) cream. Season to taste.

6 Heat the soup until completely warmed through. Transfer the soup to a tureen or to warm soup bowls and serve with crusty brown bread.

COOK'S TIP

The heads, tails, trimmings and bones of most non-oily fish can be used to make fish stock. Simmer 900 g/2 lb fish pieces in a pan with 150 ml/5 fl oz white wine, 1 chopped onion, 1 sliced carrot, 1 sliced celery stick (stalk), 4 black peppercorns, 1 bouquet garni and 1.75 litres/3 pints/7^1/2 cups water for 30 minutes, then strain.

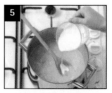

Mediterranean-style Fish Soup

Serves 4

INGREDIENTS

1 tbsp olive oil
1 large onion, chopped
2 garlic cloves, finely chopped
425 ml/15 fl oz/1³/₄ cups
    fresh fish stock
150 ml/5 fl oz/²/₃ cup dry
    white wine
1 bay leaf
1 sprig each fresh thyme,
    rosemary and oregano

450 g/1 lb firm white fish
    fillets (such as cod,
    monkfish or halibut),
    skinned and cut into
    2.5 cm/1 inch cubes
450 g/1 lb fresh mussels,
    prepared
400 g/14 oz can chopped
    tomatoes

225 g/8 oz peeled prawns
    (shrimp), thawed if frozen
salt and pepper
sprigs of thyme, to garnish

TO SERVE:
lemon wedges
4 slices toasted French bread,
    rubbed with cut garlic
    clove

---

1 Heat the oil in a large pan and gently fry the onion and garlic for 2–3 minutes until just softened.

2 Pour in the stock and wine and bring to the boil. Tie the bay leaf and herbs together with clean string and add to the saucepan together with the fish and mussels. Stir well, cover and simmer for 5 minutes.

3 Stir in the tomatoes and prawns (shrimp) and continue to cook for a further 3–4 minutes until piping hot and the fish is cooked through.

4 Discard the herbs and any mussels that have not opened. Season and ladle into warm bowls. Garnish with sprigs of thyme and serve with lemon wedges and toasted bread.

COOK'S TIP

Traditionally, the toasted bread is placed at the bottom of the bowl and the soup spooned over the top. For convenience, look out for prepared, cooked shellfish mixtures, which you could use instead of fresh fish. Simply add to the soup with the tomatoes in step 3.

Fish Soup with Wontons

Serves 4

INGREDIENTS

125 g/4 1/2 oz large, cooked, peeled prawns (shrimp)
1 tsp chopped chives
1 small garlic clove, finely chopped
1 tbsp vegetable oil

12 wonton wrappers
1 small egg, beaten
850 ml/1 1/2 pints/3 3/4 cups fish stock
175 g/6 oz white fish fillet, diced

dash of chilli sauce
sliced fresh red chilli and chives, to garnish

---

1 Roughly chop a quarter of the prawns (shrimp) and mix together with the chopped chives and garlic.

2 Heat the oil in a preheated wok and stir-fry the prawn (shrimp) mixture for 1–2 minutes. Remove from the heat and set aside to cool completely.

3 Spread out the wonton wrappers on a work surface (counter). Spoon a little of the prawn (shrimp) filling into the centre of each wonton wrapper. Brush the edges of the wonton wrappers with beaten egg and press the edges together, scrunching them to form a 'moneybag' shape. Set aside while you are preparing the soup.

4 Pour the fish stock into a large saucepan and bring to the boil. Add the diced white fish and the remaining prawns (shrimp) and cook for 5 minutes.

5 Season to taste with the chilli sauce. Add the wontons and cook for a further 5 minutes. Spoon into warmed serving bowls, garnish with sliced red chilli and chives and serve immediately.

VARIATION

Replace the prawns (shrimp) with cooked crabmeat for an alternative flavour.

Crab & Ginger Soup

Serves 4

INGREDIENTS

1 carrot, chopped
1 leek, chopped
1 bay leaf
850 ml/1¹/₂ pints/3³/₄ cups
    fish stock

2 medium-sized cooked crabs
2.5-cm/1-inch piece fresh root
    ginger (ginger root), grated
1 tsp light soy sauce

¹/₂ tsp ground star anise
salt and pepper

1 Put the carrot, leek, bay leaf and stock into a large pan and bring to the boil. Reduce the heat, cover and simmer for 10 minutes, or until the vegetables are nearly tender.

2 Meanwhile, remove all of the meat from the cooked crabs. Break off the claws, break the joints and remove the meat (you may require a fork or skewer for this). Add the crabmeat to the saucepan of fish stock.

3 Add the ginger, soy sauce and star anise to the fish stock and bring to the boil. Leave to simmer for about 10 minutes, or until the vegetables are tender and the crab is heated through. Season.

4 Ladle the soup into warmed serving bowls and garnish with crab claws. Serve at once.

COOK'S TIP

If fresh crabmeat is unavailable, use drained canned crabmeat or thawed frozen crabmeat instead.

COOK'S TIP

To prepare cooked crab, loosen the meat from the shell by banging the back of the underside with a clenched fist. Stand the crab on its edge with the shell towards you. Force the shell from the body with your thumbs. Twist off the legs and claws and remove the meat. Twist off the tail; discard. Remove and discard the gills. Cut the body in half along the centre and remove the meat. Scoop the brown meat from the shell with a spoon.

Shrimp Dumpling Soup

Serves 4

INGREDIENTS

DUMPLINGS:
150 g/5^1/$_2$ oz/1^5/$_8$ cups plain
  (all-purpose) flour
50 ml/2 fl oz/^{1}/$_4$ cup boiling
  water
25 ml/1 fl oz/^{1}/$_8$ cup cold
  water
1^1/$_2$ tsp vegetable oil

FILLING:
125 g/4^1/$_2$ oz minced (ground)
  pork
125 g/4^1/$_2$ oz cooked peeled
  shrimp, chopped
50 g/1^3/$_4$ oz canned water
  chestnuts, drained, rinsed
  and chopped
1 celery stick, chopped
1 tsp cornflour (cornstarch)

1 tbsp sesame oil
1 tbsp light soy sauce

SOUP:
850 ml/1^1/$_2$ pints/3^3/$_4$ cups
  fish stock
50 g/1^3/$_4$ oz cellophane
  noodles
1 tbsp dry sherry
chopped chives, to garnish

1 To make the dumplings, mix the flour, boiling water, cold water and oil in a bowl until a pliable dough is formed.

2 Knead the dough on a floured surface for 5 minutes. Cut the dough into 16 equal-sized pieces.

3 Roll the dough pieces into rounds 7.5 cm/ 3 inches in diameter.

4 Mix the filling ingredients together.

5 Spoon a little of the filling mixture into the centre of each round. Bring the edges of the dough together, scrunching them up to form a 'moneybag' shape. Twist to seal.

6 Pour the fish stock into a large saucepan and bring to the boil.

7 Add the cellophane noodles, dumplings and dry sherry to the pan and cook for 4–5 minutes, until the noodles and dumplings are tender. Garnish and serve.

COOK'S TIP

Wonton wrappers may be used instead of the dumpling dough if time is short.

Provençal-style Mussels

Serves 4

INGREDIENTS
---

1 tbsp olive oil
1 large onion, finely chopped
1 garlic clove, finely chopped
1 small red (bell) pepper,
    deseeded and finely
    chopped
sprig of rosemary
2 bay leaves
400 g/14 oz can chopped
    tomatoes

150 ml/5 fl oz/^{2}/$_3$ cup white
    wine
1 courgette (zucchini), diced
    finely
2 tbsp tomato purée (paste)
1 tsp caster (superfine) sugar
50 g/1^3/$_4$ oz pitted black olives
    in brine, drained and
    chopped

675 g/1^1/$_2$ lb cooked New
    Zealand mussels in their
    shells
1 tsp orange rind
salt and pepper
2 tbsp chopped, fresh parsley,
    to garnish
crusty bread, to serve

1 Heat the oil in a large saucepan and gently fry the onion, garlic and (bell) pepper for 3–4 minutes until just softened.

2 Add the sprig of rosemary and the bay leaves to the saucepan with the tomatoes and 100 ml/ 3½ fl oz/⅓ cup wine. Season to taste, then bring to the boil and simmer for 15 minutes.

3 Stir in the courgette (zucchini), tomato purée (paste), sugar and olives. Simmer for about 10 minutes.

4 Meanwhile, bring a pan of water to the boil. Arrange the mussels in a steamer or a large sieve (strainer) and place over the water. Sprinkle with the remaining wine and the orange rind. Cover and steam until the mussels open (discard any that remain closed).

5 Remove the mussels with a slotted spoon and arrange on a warm serving plate. Discard the herbs and spoon the sauce over the mussels. Garnish with chopped fresh parsley and serve with fresh, crusty bread.

Fish & Rice with Dark Rum

Serves 4

INGREDIENTS

450 g/1 lb firm white fish
  fillets (such as cod or
  monkfish), skinned and cut
  into 2.5 cm/1 inch cubes
2 tsp ground cumin
2 tsp dried oregano
2 tbsp lime juice
150 ml/5 fl oz/²/3 cup dark
  rum
1 tbsp dark muscovado sugar
3 garlic cloves, chopped finely

1 large onion, chopped
1 medium red (bell) pepper,
  deseeded and sliced into
  rings
1 medium green (bell) pepper,
  deseeded and sliced into
  rings
1 medium yellow (bell) pepper,
  deseeded and sliced into
  rings

1.2 litres/2 pints/5 cups fish
  stock
350 g/12 oz/2 cups long-grain
  rice
salt and pepper
crusty bread, to serve

TO GARNISH:
fresh oregano leaves
lime wedges

---

1 Place the cubes of fish in a bowl and add the cumin, oregano, salt and pepper, lime juice, rum and sugar. Mix well, cover and leave to chill for 2 hours.

2 Place the garlic, onion and (bell) peppers in a large pan. Pour over the stock and stir in the rice. Bring to the boil, cover and cook for 15 minutes.

3 Gently add the fish and the marinade juices to the pan. Bring back to the boil and simmer, uncovered, stirring occasionally but taking care not to break up the fish, for 10 minutes until the fish is cooked and the rice is just tender.

4 Season with salt and pepper to taste and transfer to a warm serving plate. Garnish with fresh oregano and lime wedges and serve with crusty bread.

VARIATION

If you prefer, use unsweetened orange juice in the marinade instead of the rum.

Smoky Fish Pie

Serves 4

INGREDIENTS

900 g/2 lb smoked haddock or cod fillets	115 g/4 oz frozen peas	60 g/2 oz smoked salmon, sliced into thin strips
600 ml/1 pint/2½ cups skimmed milk	115 g/4 oz frozen sweetcorn kernels	3 tbsp cornflour (cornstarch)
2 bay leaves	675 g/1½ lb potatoes, diced	25 g/1 oz smoked cheese, grated
115 g/4 oz button mushrooms, quartered	5 tbsp low-fat natural (unsweetened) yogurt	salt and pepper
	4 tbsp chopped fresh parsley	

1 Preheat the oven to 200°C/400°F/Gas Mark 6. Place the fish in a pan and add the milk and bay leaves. Bring to the boil, cover and then simmer for 5 minutes.

2 Add the mushrooms, peas and sweetcorn to the pan, bring back to a simmer, cover and cook for 5–7 minutes. Leave to cool.

3 Place the potatoes in a pan, cover with water, boil and cook for 8 minutes.

Drain and mash with a fork or a potato masher. Stir in the yogurt, parsley and seasoning. Set aside.

4 Using a slotted spoon, remove the fish from the pan. Flake the cooked fish away from the skin and place in an ovenproof gratin dish. Reserve the cooking liquid.

5 Drain the vegetables, reserving the cooking liquid, and stir into the fish with the salmon strips.

6 Blend a little cooking liquid into the cornflour (cornstarch) to make a paste. Transfer the rest of the liquid to a pan and add the paste. Heat through, stirring, until thickened. Discard the bay leaves and season to taste.

7 Pour the sauce over the fish and vegetables. Spoon over the mashed potato so that the fish is covered, sprinkle with cheese and bake for 25–30 minutes. Serve.

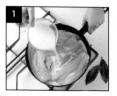

Seafood Spaghetti

Serves 4

INGREDIENTS
---

2 tsp olive oil
1 small red onion, chopped finely
1 tbsp lemon juice
1 garlic clove, crushed
2 sticks celery, chopped finely
150 ml/5 fl oz/^{2}/$_3$ cup fresh fish stock

150 ml/5 fl oz/^{2}/$_3$ cup dry white wine
small bunch fresh tarragon
450 g/1 lb fresh mussels, prepared
225 g/8 oz fresh prawns (shrimp), peeled and deveined

225 g/8 oz baby squid, cleaned, trimmed and sliced into rings
8 small cooked crab claws, cracked and peeled
225 g/8 oz spaghetti
salt and pepper
2 tbsp chopped fresh tarragon, to garnish

---

1 Heat the oil in a large pan and fry the onion with the lemon juice, garlic and celery for 3–4 minutes until just softened.

2 Pour in the stock and wine. Bring to the boil and add the tarragon and mussels. Cover and simmer for 5 minutes. Add the prawns (shrimp), squid and crab claws to the pan, mix and cook for 3–4 minutes until the mussels

have opened, the prawns (shrimp) are pink and the squid is opaque. Discard any mussels that have not opened and the tarragon.

3 Meanwhile, cook the spaghetti in a saucepan of boiling water according to the instructions on the packet. Drain well.

4 Add the spaghetti to the shellfish mixture and toss together. Season.

5 Transfer to warm serving plates and spoon over the cooking juices. Serve garnished with freshly chopped tarragon.

COOK'S TIP

Crab claws contain lean crab meat. Ask your fishmonger to crack the claws for you, leaving the pincers intact, because the shell is very tough.

Chilli- & Crab-stuffed Red Snapper

Serves 4

INGREDIENTS

4 red snappers, cleaned and
  scaled, 175 g/6 oz each
2 tbsp dry sherry
salt and pepper
stir-fried shredded vegetables,
  to serve

STUFFING:
1 small red chilli
1 garlic clove
1 spring onion (scallion)
$1/2$ tsp finely grated lime rind
1 tbsp lime juice

100 g/$3^1/2$ oz white crab meat,
  flaked

TO GARNISH:
wedges of lime
red chilli strips

---

1 Rinse the fish and pat dry on absorbent kitchen paper. Season inside and out and place in a shallow dish. Spoon over the sherry and set aside.

2 Meanwhile, make the stuffing. Carefully halve, deseed and finely chop the chilli. Place in a small bowl.

3 Peel and finely chop the garlic. Trim and finely chop the spring onion (scallion). Add to the chilli together with the grated lime rind, lime juice and the flaked crab meat. Season with salt and pepper to taste and combine. Spoon some of the stuffing into the cavity of each fish.

4 Bring a large pan of water to the boil. Arrange the fish in a steamer lined with baking parchment or in a large sieve (strainer) and place over the boiling water. Cover and steam for 10 minutes. Turn the fish over and steam for 10 minutes or until the fish is cooked.

5 Drain the fish and transfer to serving plates. Garnish with wedges of lime and serve with stir-fried vegetables.

COOK'S TIP

Always wash your hands thoroughly after handling chillies as they can irritate your skin and eyes.

Seafood Pizza

Serves 4

INGREDIENTS

145 g/5 oz standard pizza base
   mix
4 tbsp chopped fresh dill or
   2 tbsp dried dill
fresh dill, to garnish

SAUCE:
1 large red (bell) pepper

400 g/14 oz can chopped
   tomatoes with onion and
   herbs
3 tbsp tomato purée (paste)
salt and pepper

TOPPING:
350 g/12 oz assorted cooked
   seafood, thawed if frozen

1 tbsp capers in brine, drained
25 g/1 oz pitted black olives in
   brine, drained
25 g/1 oz low-fat Mozzarella
   cheese, grated
1 tbsp grated, fresh Parmesan
   cheese

1 Preheat the oven to 200°C/400°F/Gas Mark 6. Place the pizza base mix in a bowl and stir in the dill. Make the dough according to the instructions on the packet.

2 Press the dough into a round measuring 25.5 cm/10 inches across on a baking sheet (cookie sheet) lined with baking parchment. Set aside to prove (rise).

3 Preheat the grill (broiler) to hot. To make the sauce, halve and deseed the (bell) pepper and arrange on a grill (broiler) rack. Cook for 8–10 minutes until softened and charred. Leave to cool slightly, peel off the skin and chop the flesh.

4 Place the tomatoes and (bell) pepper in a saucepan. Bring to the boil and simmer for 10 minutes.

Stir in the tomato purée (paste) and season to taste.

5 Spread the sauce over the pizza base and top with the seafood. Sprinkle over the capers and olives, top with the grated cheeses and bake for 25–30 minutes. Garnish with sprigs of dill and serve hot.

Pan-seared Halibut
with Red Onion Relish

Serves 4

INGREDIENTS

1 tsp olive oil
4 halibut steaks, skinned,
    175 g/6 oz each
1/2 tsp cornflour (cornstarch)
    mixed with 2 tsp cold
    water
salt and pepper

2 tbsp fresh chives, snipped,
    to garnish

RED ONION RELISH:
2 medium red onions
6 shallots
1 tbsp lemon juice

2 tsp olive oil
2 tbsp red wine vinegar
2 tsp caster (superfine) sugar
150 ml/5 fl oz/2/3 cup fresh
    fish stock

1 To make the relish, peel and thinly shred the onions and shallots. Place in a small bowl and toss in the lemon juice.

2 Heat the oil in a pan and fry the onions and shallots for 3–4 minutes until just softened.

3 Add the vinegar and sugar and continue to cook for a further 2 minutes over a high heat.

Pour in the stock and season well. Bring to the boil and simmer gently for a further 8–9 minutes until the sauce has thickened and is slightly reduced.

4 Brush a non-stick, ridged frying pan (skillet) with oil and heat until hot. Press the fish steaks into the pan to seal, lower the heat and cook for 4 minutes. Turn the fish over and cook for 4–5

minutes until cooked through. Drain on kitchen paper and keep warm.

5 Stir the cornflour (cornstarch) paste into the onion sauce and heat through, stirring, until thickened. Season to taste.

6 Pile the relish on to 4 warm serving plates and place a halibut steak on top of each. Garnish with chives and pepper.

Baked Trout Mexican-style

Serves 4

INGREDIENTS

4 trout, 225 g/8 oz each
1 small bunch fresh coriander (cilantro)
4 shallots, shredded finely
1 small yellow (bell) pepper, deseeded and very finely chopped

1 small red (bell) pepper, deseeded and very finely chopped
2 green chillies, deseeded and finely chopped
1–2 red chillies, deseeded and finely chopped

1 tbsp lemon juice
1 tbsp white wine vinegar
2 tsp caster (superfine) sugar
salt and pepper
fresh coriander (cilantro), to garnish
salad leaves, to serve

1 Preheat the oven to 180°C/350°F/Gas Mark 4. Wash the trout and pat dry with absorbent kitchen paper. Season the cavities with salt and pepper and fill with a few coriander (cilantro) leaves.

2 Place the fish side by side in a shallow ovenproof dish. Sprinkle over the shallots, (bell) peppers and chillies.

3 Mix together the lemon juice, vinegar and sugar in a bowl. Spoon over the trout and season to taste. Cover the dish and bake for 30 minutes or until the fish is tender and the flesh is opaque.

4 Remove the fish with a fish slice and drain. Transfer to warm serving plates and spoon the cooking juices over the fish. Garnish with fresh coriander (cilantro) and serve immediately with chilli bean rice, if you wish (see Cook's Tip, right).

COOK'S TIP

To make chilli bean rice to serve with this recipe, cook 225 g/8 oz/1¼ cup long-grain white rice in boiling water. Drain and return to the pan. Drain and rinse a 400 g/14 oz can kidney beans and stir into the rice along with 1 tsp each of ground cumin and ground coriander. Stir in 4 tbsp freshly chopped coriander (cilantro) and season well.

Fried Fish in Gram Flour

Serves 4-6

INGREDIENTS

100 g/3¹/₂ oz/³/₄ cup gram flour	¹/₂ tsp turmeric	300 ml/¹/₂ pint/1¹/₄ cups oil
1 tsp fresh ginger root, finely chopped	2 fresh green chillies, chopped	cooked rice, to serve
1 tsp fresh garlic, crushed	fresh coriander (cilantro) leaves, chopped	TO GARNISH:
2 tsp chilli powder	300 ml/¹/₂ pint/1¹/₄ cups water	2 lemons, cut into wedges
1 tsp salt	1 kg/2 lb 4 oz cod	6 green chillies, slit down the middle

1 Place the gram flour in a large mixing bowl. Add the ginger, garlic, chilli powder, salt and turmeric and mix to blend well.

2 Add the green chillies and the coriander (cilantro) leaves to the spiced mixture and stir to mix well.

3 Pour in the water gradually and stir thoroughly to form a semi-thick batter. Set aside until it is required.

4 Using a sharp knife, cut the cod into about 8 pieces.

5 Carefully dip the pieces of cod into the batter, coating the cod all over. Gently shake off any excess batter.

6 Heat the oil in a heavy-based frying-pan (skillet). Add the battered cod and fry, in batches, over a medium heat, turning once, until cooked through and golden.

7 Transfer the battered cod to a serving dish and garnish with lemon wedges and green chillies. Serve with cooked rice.

COOK'S TIP

Gram flour or chana dhaal flour (lentil flour) is used to make Pakoras and to bind kebabs (kabobs). Combined with ordinary wholemeal flour it makes a delicious Indian bread.

Bengali-Style Fish

Serves 4-6

INGREDIENTS

1 tsp turmeric
1 tsp salt
1 kg/2 lb 4 oz cod fillet,
    skinned and cut into pieces
6 tbsp corn oil

4 green chillies
1 tsp fresh ginger root, finely
    chopped
1 tsp fresh garlic, crushed
2 medium onions, finely
    chopped

2 tomatoes, finely chopped
6 tbsp mustard oil
450 ml/³/4 pint/2 cups water
fresh coriander (cilantro)
    leaves, chopped, to garnish

1 Mix together the turmeric and salt in a small bowl.

2 Spoon the turmeric and salt mixture over the fish pieces.

3 Heat the oil in a frying-pan (skillet) and fry the fish pieces until pale yellow. Remove the fish with a perforated spoon and set aside.

4 Place the green chillies, ginger, garlic, onions, tomatoes and mustard oil in a pestle and mortar and grind to form a paste. Alternatively, work the ingredients in a food processor.

5 Transfer the spice paste to a saucepan and dry-fry until golden brown.

6 Remove the pan from the heat and gently place the fish pieces into the paste without breaking the fish up.

7 Return the pan to the heat, add the water and cook the fish, uncovered, over a medium heat for 15-20 minutes.

8 Garnish with chopped coriander (cilantro).

COOK'S TIP

In the hot and humid eastern plains that surround Bengal, the mustard plant flourishes, providing oil for cooking and spicy seeds for flavouring. Fish and seafood appear in many meals, often flavoured with mustard oil.

Prawns (Shrimp) with Spinach

Serves 4-6

INGREDIENTS

225 g/8 oz frozen prawns (shrimp)	2 tomatoes	1 tsp fresh ginger root, finely chopped
350 g/12 oz canned spinach purée or frozen spinach, thawed and chopped	150 ml/¹/₄ pint/²/₃ cup oil ¹/₂ tsp mustard seeds ¹/₂ tsp onion seeds	1 tsp fresh garlic, crushed 1 tsp chilli powder 1 tsp salt

1 Place the prawns (shrimp) in a bowl of cold water and set aside to defrost thoroughly.

2 Drain the can of spinach purée, if using.

3 Using a sharp knife, cut the tomatoes into slices and set aside.

4 Heat the oil in a large frying pan (skillet). Add the mustard and onion seeds to the pan.

5 Reduce the heat and add the tomatoes, spinach, ginger, garlic, chilli powder and salt to the pan and stir-fry for about 5-7 minutes.

6 Drain the prawns (shrimp) thoroughly.

7 Add the prawns (shrimp) to the spinach mixture in the pan. Gently stir the prawn (shrimp) and spinach mixture until well combined, cover and leave to simmer over a low heat for about 7-10 minutes.

8 Transfer the cooked prawns (shrimp) and spinach to a serving dish and serve hot.

COOK'S TIP

If using frozen spinach, it should be thawed and squeezed dry before using. You could use fresh spinach, if you prefer.

Prawns (Shrimp) with Tomatoes

Serves 4-6

INGREDIENTS

3 medium onions
1 green (bell) pepper
1 tsp fresh ginger root, finely
   chopped
1 tsp fresh garlic, crushed

1 tsp salt
1 tsp chilli powder
2 tbsp lemon juice
350 g/12 oz frozen prawns
   (shrimp)

3 tbsp oil
400 g/14 oz can tomatoes
fresh coriander (cilantro)
   leaves, to garnish

1 Using a sharp knife, slice the onions and the green (bell) pepper.

2 Place the ginger, garlic, salt and chilli powder in a small bowl and mix. Add the lemon juice and mix to form a paste.

3 Place the prawns (shrimp) in a bowl of cold water and set aside to defrost. Drain thoroughly.

4 Heat the oil in a medium-sized saucepan. Add the onions and fry until golden brown.

5 Add the spice paste to the onions, reduce the heat to low and cook, stirring and mixing well, for about 3 minutes.

6 Add the tomatoes, tomato juice and the green (bell) pepper, and cook for 5-7 minutes, stirring occasionally.

7 Add the defrosted prawns (shrimp) to the pan and cook the mixture for about 10 minutes, stirring occasionally. Garnish with fresh coriander (cilantro) leaves

and serve hot with plain boiled rice and a crisp green salad.

COOK'S TIP

Fresh ginger root looks rather like a knobbly potato. The skin should be peeled, then the flesh either grated, finely chopped or sliced. Ginger is also available ground: this can be used as a substitute for fresh root ginger, but the fresh root is far superior.

Steamed Fish with Black Bean Sauce

Serves 4

INGREDIENTS

900 g/2 lb whole snapper,
  cleaned and scaled
3 garlic cloves, crushed
2 tbsp black bean sauce
1 tsp cornflour (cornstarch)

2 tsp sesame oil
2 tbsp light soy sauce
2 tsp caster (superfine) sugar
2 tbsp dry sherry
1 small leek, shredded

1 small red (bell) pepper,
  seeded and cut into thin
  strips
shredded leek and lemon
  wedges, to garnish
boiled rice or noodles, to serve

1 Rinse the fish inside and out with cold running water and pat dry with kitchen paper (paper towels). Make 2-3 diagonal slashes in the flesh on each side of the fish, using a sharp knife. Rub the garlic into the fish.

2 Thoroughly mix the black bean sauce, cornflour (cornstarch), sesame oil, light soy sauce, sugar and dry sherry together in a bowl. Place the fish in a shallow heatproof dish and pour the sauce mixture over the top.

3 Sprinkle the leek and (bell) pepper strips on top of the sauce. Place the dish in the top of a steamer, cover and steam for 10 minutes, or until the fish is cooked through.

4 Transfer to a serving dish, garnish with shredded leek and lemon wedges and serve with boiled rice or noodles.

VARIATION

Whole sea bream or sea bass may be used in this recipe instead of snapper, if you prefer.

COOK'S TIP

Insert the point of a sharp knife into the fish to test if it is cooked. The fish is cooked through if the knife goes into the flesh easily.

Mullet with Ginger

Serves 4

INGREDIENTS

1 whole mullet, cleaned and scaled
2 spring onions (scallions), chopped
1 tsp grated fresh root ginger
125 ml/4 fl oz/¹/2 cup garlic wine vinegar

125 ml/4 fl oz/¹/2 cup light soy sauce
3 tsp caster (superfine) sugar
dash of chilli sauce
125 ml/4 fl oz/¹/2 cup fish stock
1 green (bell) pepper, seeded and thinly sliced

1 large tomato, skinned, seeded and cut into thin strips
salt and pepper
sliced tomato, to garnish

1 Rinse the fish inside and out and pat dry with kitchen paper (paper towels).

2 Make 3 diagonal slits in the flesh on each side of the fish. Season with salt and pepper inside and out.

3 Place the fish on a heatproof plate and scatter the spring onions (scallions) and ginger over the top. Cover and steam for 10 minutes, or until the fish is cooked through.

4 Place the vinegar, soy sauce, sugar, chilli sauce, fish stock, (bell) pepper and tomato in a saucepan and bring to the boil, stirring occasionally. Cook over a high heat until the sauce has slightly reduced and thickened.

5 Remove the fish from the steamer and transfer to a warm serving dish. Pour the sauce over the fish, garnish with tomato slices and serve immediately.

COOK'S TIP

Use fillets of fish for this recipe if preferred, and reduce the cooking time to 5–7 minutes.

Szechuan White Fish

Serves 4

INGREDIENTS

---

350 g/12 oz white fish fillets
1 small egg, beaten
3 tbsp plain (all-purpose) flour
4 tbsp dry white wine
3 tbsp light soy sauce
vegetable oil, for frying
1 garlic clove, cut into slivers
1-cm/¹/₂-inch piece fresh root
    ginger, finely chopped

1 onion, finely chopped
1 celery stick, chopped
1 fresh red chilli, chopped
3 spring onions (scallions),
    chopped
1 tsp rice wine vinegar
¹/₂ tsp ground Szechuan
    pepper

175 ml/6 fl oz/³/₄ cup fish
    stock
1 tsp caster (superfine) sugar
1 tsp cornflour (cornstarch)
2 tsp water
chilli flowers and celery leaves,
    to garnish (optional)

---

1 Cut the fish into 4-cm/ 1¹/₂-inch cubes.

2 In a bowl, beat the egg, flour, wine and 1 tbsp of soy sauce to make a batter.

3 Dip the cubes of fish into the batter to coat.

4 Heat the oil in a preheated wok until it is almost smoking. Reduce the heat slightly and cook the fish, in batches, for

2–3 minutes, until golden. Drain on kitchen paper (paper towels) and set aside.

5 Pour all but 1 tbsp of oil from the wok and return to the heat. Add the garlic, ginger, onion, celery, chilli and spring onions (scallions) and stir-fry for 1–2 minutes.

6 Stir in the remaining soy sauce and the vinegar.

7 Add the Szechuan pepper, fish stock and sugar to the wok. Blend the cornflour (cornstarch) with the water to form a smooth paste and stir it into the stock. Bring to the boil and cook, stirring, for 1 minute, until the sauce thickens and clears.

8 Return the fish to the wok and cook for 1–2 minutes, until hot. Transfer to a serving dish.

(Small) Shrimp Fu Yong

Serves 4

INGREDIENTS

2 tbsp vegetable oil
1 carrot, grated
5 eggs, beaten
225 g/8 oz (small) shrimp, peeled

1 tbsp light soy sauce
pinch of Chinese five spice powder
2 spring onions (scallions), chopped

2 tsp sesame seeds
1 tsp sesame oil

1 Heat the vegetable oil in a preheated wok.

2 Add the carrot and stir-fry for 1–2 minutes.

3 Push the carrot to one side of the wok and add the eggs. Cook, stirring gently, for 1–2 minutes.

4 Stir the (small) shrimp, soy sauce and five spice powder into the mixture in the wok. Stir-fry the mixture for 2–3 minutes, or until the (small) shrimps change colour and the mixture is almost dry.

5 Turn the (small) shrimp fu yong out on to a warm plate and sprinkle the spring onions (scallions), sesame seeds and sesame oil on top. Serve immediately.

VARIATION

For a more substantial dish, you could add 225 g/8 oz/ 1 cup cooked long-grain rice with the (small) shrimp in step 4. Taste and adjust the quantities of soy sauce, Chinese five spice powder and sesame oil if necessary.

COOK'S TIP

If only cooked prawns (shrimp) are available, add them just before the end of cooking, but make sure that they are fully incorporated into the fu yong. They require only heating through – overcooking will make them chewy and tasteless.

Squid With Oyster Sauce

Serves 4

INGREDIENTS

450 g/1 lb squid	60 g/2 oz mangetout (snow peas)	SAUCE:
150 ml/¹/₄ pint/²/₃ cup vegetable oil	5 tbsp hot fish stock	1 tbsp oyster sauce
1-cm/¹/₂-inch piece fresh root ginger, grated	red (bell) pepper triangles, to garnish	1 tbsp light soy sauce
		pinch of caster (superfine) sugar
		1 garlic clove, crushed

1 To prepare the squid, cut down the centre of the body lengthways. Flatten the squid out, inside uppermost, and score a lattice design deep into the flesh, using a sharp knife.

2 To make the sauce, combine the oyster sauce, soy sauce, sugar and garlic in a small bowl. Stir to dissolve the sugar and set aside until required.

3 Heat the oil in a preheated wok until almost smoking. Lower the heat slightly, add the squid and stir-fry until they curl up. Remove with a slotted spoon and drain thoroughly on kitchen paper (paper towels).

4 Pour off all but 2 tablespoons of the oil and return the wok to the heat. Add the ginger and mangetout (snow peas) and stir-fry for 1 minute.

5 Return the squid to the wok and pour in the sauce and hot fish stock.

Leave the mixture to simmer for 3 minutes, or until thickened.

6 Transfer to a warm serving dish, garnish with (bell) pepper triangles and serve immediately.

COOK'S TIP

Take care not to overcook the squid, otherwise it will be rubbery and unappetizing.

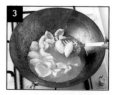

Crab in Ginger Sauce

Serves 4

INGREDIENTS

2 small cooked crabs
2 tbsp vegetable oil
9-cm/3-inch piece fresh root ginger, grated
2 garlic cloves, thinly sliced

1 green (bell) pepper, seeded and cut into thin strips
6 spring onions (scallions), cut into 2.5-cm/1-inch lengths
2 tbsp dry sherry

$^1/_2$ tsp sesame oil
150 ml/$^1/_4$ pint/$^2/_3$ cup fish stock
1 tsp light brown sugar
2 tsp cornflour (cornstarch)
150 ml/$^1/_4$ pint/$^2/_3$ cup water

1 Rinse the crabs and gently loosen around the shell at the top. Using a sharp knife, cut away the grey tissue and discard. Rinse the crabs again.

2 Twist off the legs and claws from the crabs. Using a pair of crab claw crackers or a cleaver, crack the claws to break through the shell to expose the flesh. Remove and discard any loose pieces of shell.

3 Separate the body and discard the inedible

lungs and sac. Cut down the centre of each crab to separate the body into two pieces and then cut each of these in half again.

4 Heat the oil in a preheated wok. Add the ginger and garlic and stir-fry for 1 minute. Add the crab pieces and stir-fry for 1 minute.

5 Stir in the (bell) pepper, spring onions (scallions), sherry, sesame oil, stock and sugar. Bring to the boil, reduce the heat,

cover and simmer for 3–4 minutes.

6 Blend the cornflour (cornstarch) with the remaining water and stir it into the wok. Bring to the boil, stirring, until the sauce is thickened and clear. Serve.

COOK'S TIP

If preferred, remove the crabmeat from the shells prior to stir-frying and add to the wok with the (bell) pepper.

Indonesian-style Spicy Cod

Serves 4

INGREDIENTS

4 cod steaks
1 stalk lemon grass
1 small red onion, chopped
3 cloves garlic, chopped
2 fresh red chillies, deseeded
    and chopped

1 tsp grated root (fresh)
    ginger
$1/4$ tsp turmeric
2 tbsp butter, cut into small
    cubes
8 tbsp canned coconut milk

2 tbsp lemon juice
salt and pepper
red chillies, to garnish
    (optional)

1 Rinse the cod steaks and pat them thoroughly dry on absorbent kitchen paper.

2 Remove and discard the outer leaves from the lemon grass and thinly slice the inner section.

3 Place the lemon grass, onion, garlic, chilli, ginger and turmeric in a food processor and blend until the ingredients are finely chopped. Season with salt and pepper to taste.

4 With the processor running, add the butter, coconut milk and lemon juice and process until well blended.

5 Place the fish in a shallow, non-metallic dish. Pour over the coconut mixture and turn the fish until well coated.

6 If you have one, place the fish steaks in a hinged basket, which will make them easier to turn. Barbecue (grill) over hot coals for 15 minutes or

until the fish is cooked through, turning once. Serve garnished with red chillies, if wished.

COOK'S TIP

If you prefer a milder flavour omit the chillies altogether. For a hotter flavour do not remove the seeds from the chillies.

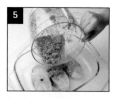

Salmon Yakitori

Serves 4

INGREDIENTS

350 g/12 oz chunky salmon fillet 8 baby leeks	YAKITORI SAUCE: 5 tbsp light soy sauce 5 tbsp fish stock 2 tbsp caster (superfine) sugar	5 tbsp dry white wine 3 tbsp sweet sherry 1 clove garlic, crushed

1 Skin the salmon and cut the flesh into 5 cm/2 inch chunks. Trim the leeks and cut them into 5 cm/2 inch lengths.

2 Thread the salmon and leeks alternately on to 8 pre-soaked wooden skewers. Leave to chill in the refrigerator until required.

3 To make the sauce, place all of the ingredients in a small pan and heat gently, stirring, until the sugar dissolves. Bring to the boil, then reduce the heat and simmer for 2 minutes. Strain the sauce and leave to cool.

4 Pour about one-third of the sauce into a small dish and set aside to serve with the kebabs (kabobs).

5 Brush plenty of the remaining sauce over the skewers and cook directly on the rack or, if preferred, place a sheet of oiled kitchen foil on the rack and cook the salmon on that. Barbecue (grill) the skewers over hot coals for about 10 minutes, turning once. Baste frequently during cooking with the remaining sauce to prevent the fish and vegetables from drying out. Serve the kebebs (kabobs) with the reserved sauce for dipping.

COOK'S TIP

Soak the wooden skewers in cold water for at least 30 minutes to prevent them from burning during cooking. You can make the kebabs (kabobs) and sauce several hours before required and refrigerate.

Japanese-style Char-grilled Plaice (Flounder)

Serves 4

INGREDIENTS

4 small plaice (flounders)
6 tbsp soy sauce
2 tbsp sake or dry white wine
2 tbsp sesame oil
1 tbsp lemon juice

2 tbsp light muscovado sugar
1 tsp root (fresh) ginger, grated
1 clove garlic, crushed

TO GARNISH:
1 small carrot
4 spring onions (scallion)

1 Rinse the fish and pat them dry on absorbent kitchen paper. Cut a few slashes into both sides of each fish.

2 Mix together the soy sauce, sake or wine, oil, lemon juice, sugar, ginger and garlic in a large, shallow dish.

3 Place the fish in the marinade and turn so that they are coated on both sides. Chill in the refrigerator for 1–6 hours.

4 Meanwhile, prepare the garnish. Cut the carrot into evenly-sized thin sticks and clean and shred the spring onions (scallions).

5 Barbecue (grill) the fish over hot coals for about 10 minutes, turning the fish once.

6 Scatter the spring onions (scallions) and carrot over the fish and transfer the fish to a serving dish. Serve immediately.

VARIATION

Use sole instead of the plaice (flounders) and scatter over some toasted sesame seeds instead of the carrot and spring onions (scallions), if you prefer.

Mackerel with Lime & Coriander (Cilantro)

Serves 4

INGREDIENTS

4 small mackerel, trout or
    sardines
1/4 tsp ground coriander
1/4 tsp ground cumin
4 sprigs fresh coriander
    (cilantro)

3 tbsp chopped, fresh
    coriander (cilantro)
1 red chilli, deseeded and
    chopped
grated rind and juice of 1 lime
2 tbsp sunflower oil

salt and pepper
1 lime, sliced, to garnish
chilli flowers, to garnish
    (optional)
salad leaves, to serve

1 To make the chilli flowers (if using), cut the tip of a small chilli lengthwise into thin strips, leaving the chilli intact at the stem end. Remove the seeds and place in iced water until curled.

2 Clean and gut the mackerel, removing the heads if preferred. Place on a chopping board.

3 Sprinkle the fish with the ground spices and salt and pepper to taste. Place a sprig of coriander (cilantro) inside the cavity of each fish.

4 Mix together the chopped coriander (cilantro), chilli, lime rind and juice and the oil in a small bowl. Brush the mixture liberally over the fish.

5 Place the fish in a hinged rack if you have one. Barbecue (grill) the fish over hot coals for 3–4 minutes on each side, turning once. Brush frequently with the remaining basting mixture.

6 Garnish with lime slices and chilli flowers, if using, and serve with salad leaves.

Nutty Stuffed Trout

Serves 4

INGREDIENTS

4 medium trout, cleaned	rind of 1 orange, grated	oil for brushing
2 tbsp sunflower oil	2 tbsp orange juice	salt and pepper
1 small onion, chopped finely	75 g/2³/₄ oz fresh wholemeal	orange slices, to garnish
50 g/1 ³/₄ oz toasted mixed	breadcrumbs	orange and watercress salad,
nuts, chopped	1 medium egg, beaten	to serve

1 Season the trout inside and out with salt and pepper to taste.

2 To make the stuffing, heat the oil in a small saucepan and fry the onion until soft. Remove the pan from the heat and stir in the chopped nuts, grated orange rind, orange juice and the breadcrumbs. Add just enough beaten egg to bind the mixture together.

3 Divide the stuffing into 4 equal portions and spoon into the body of each fish.

4 Brush the fish liberally with oil and barbecue (grill) over medium hot coals for 10 minutes on each side, turning once. When the fish is cooked the flesh will be white and firm and the skin will be beginning to crispen.

5 Transfer the fish to individual serving plates and garnish with orange slices.

6 Serve the fish with an orange and watercress salad and an orange and mustard dressing.

COOK'S TIP

Serve the stuffed trout with an orange and watercress salad. For the dressing, mix together 2 tbsp orange juice, 1 tbsp white wine vinegar, 3 tbsp olive oil, ¹/₂ tsp wholegrain mustard and salt and pepper to taste. Pour the dressing over the orange and watercress salad just before serving.

Sardines with Olives & Tomatoes

Serves 4

INGREDIENTS

12 fresh sardines, gutted and
    cleaned
fresh basil leaves
4 plum tomatoes
8 pitted black olives

15 g/^{1}/$_2$ oz butter
1 tbsp olive oil
2 tbsp lemon juice
salt and pepper

TO GARNISH:
plum tomatoes, sliced
olives, sliced
1 fresh basil sprig

1 Season the sardines inside and out with salt and pepper to taste. Insert 1-2 basil leaves inside the cavity of each fish. Using a sharp knife, make a few slashes in the body of each fish.

2 Cut the tomatoes and olives into slices and transfer to a large bowl. Tear 4 basil leaves into small pieces and toss together with the tomatoes and olives.

3 Divide the tomato and olive mixture among

4 large sheets of kitchen foil, and place 3 sardines on top of each portion.

4 Melt the butter and oil in a small pan. Stir in the lemon juice and pour the mixture over the fish.

5 Carefully wrap up the fish in the foil. Barbecue (grill) the fish over medium hot coals for 15–20 minutes until the fish is cooked through.

6 Transfer the fish to individual serving plates and remove the foil.

Garnish the fish with slices of tomato and olive, and with a fresh sprig of basil. Serve at once.

COOK'S TIP

Slashing the body of the fish helps the flesh to absorb the flavours. It is particularly important if you do not have time to allow the fish to marinate before cooking.

Herrings with
Orange Tarragon Stuffing

Serves 4

INGREDIENTS

1 orange
4 spring onions (scallions)
50 g/1³/₄ oz fresh wholemeal
  breadcrumbs
1 tbsp fresh tarragon, chopped

4 herrings, cleaned and gutted
salt and pepper
green salad, to serve

TO GARNISH:
2 oranges
1 tbsp light brown sugar
1 tbsp olive oil
sprigs of fresh tarragon

1 To make the stuffing, grate the rind from half of the orange, using a zester.

2 Peel and chop all of the orange flesh on a plate in order to catch all of the juice.

3 Mix together the orange flesh, juice, rind, spring onions (scallions), breadcrumbs and tarragon in a bowl. Season with salt and pepper to taste.

4 Divide the stuffing into 4 equal portions and use it to fill the body cavities of the fish.

5 Place each fish on to a square of lightly greased kitchen foil and wrap the foil around the fish so that it is completely enclosed. Barbecue (grill) over hot coals for 20–30 minutes until the herrings are cooked through – their flesh should be white and firm to the touch.

6 Meanwhile make the garnish. Peel and thickly slice the 2 oranges and sprinkle over the sugar. Just before the fish is cooked, drizzle a little oil over the orange slices and place them on the barbecue for 5 minutes to heat through.

7 Transfer the fish to serving plates and garnish with the barbecued (grilled) orange slices and sprigs of fresh tarragon. Serve with a green salad.

Vermicelli with Fillets of Red Mullet

Serves 4

INGREDIENTS

1 kg/2^1/4 lb red mullet fillets	pinch of freshly grated	salt and pepper
300 ml/^{1}/2 pint/1^1/4 cups dry	nutmeg	
white wine	3 anchovy fillets, roughly	TO GARNISH:
4 shallots, finely chopped	chopped	1 fresh mint sprig
1 garlic clove, crushed	2 tbsp double (heavy) cream	lemon slices
3 tbsp mixed fresh herbs	1 tsp cornflour (cornstarch)	lemon rind
finely grated rind and juice of	450 g/1 lb dried vermicelli	
1 lemon	1 tbsp olive oil	

1 Put the red mullet fillets in a large casserole. Pour over the wine and add the shallots, garlic, herbs, lemon rind and juice, nutmeg and anchovies. Season with salt and pepper to taste. Cover and bake in a preheated oven at 180°C/350°F/Gas 4 for 35 minutes.

2 Carefully transfer the mullet and herbs to a warm dish. Set aside and keep warm.

3 Pour the cooking liquid into a pan and bring to the boil. Simmer for 25 minutes, until reduced by half. Mix the cream and cornflour (cornstarch) and stir into the sauce to thicken.

4 Bring a pan of salted water to the boil. Add the vermicelli and olive oil and cook until tender, but still firm to the bite. Drain the pasta and transfer to a warm serving dish.

5 Discard the herbs before arranging the red mullet fillets on top of the vermicelli; pour over the sauce. Garnish with a fresh mint sprig, slices of lemon and strips of lemon rind. Serve immediately.

COOK'S TIP

The best red mullet is sometimes called golden mullet, although it is bright red in colour.

Ravioli of Lemon Sole & Haddock

Serves 4

INGREDIENTS

450 g/1 lb lemon sole fillets,
skinned
450 g/1 lb haddock fillets,
skinned
3 eggs beaten
450 g/1 lb cooked potato
gnocchi

175 g/6 oz/3 cups fresh
breadcrumbs
50 ml/2 fl oz/$^1/_4$ cup double
(heavy) cream
450 g/1 lb Basic Pasta Dough

300 ml/$^1/_2$ pint/1$^1/_4$ cups
Italian Red Wine Sauce
60 g/2 oz/$^2/_3$ cup freshly
grated Parmesan cheese
salt and pepper

1 Flake the fish fillets in a large mixing bowl.

2 Mix the eggs, cooked potato gnocchi, breadcrumbs and cream in a bowl until combined. Add the fish and season the mixture to taste.

3 Roll out the pasta dough on to a lightly floured surface and cut out 7.5 cm/3 inch rounds.

4 Place a spoonful of the fish stuffing on each round. Dampen the edges slightly and fold the pasta rounds over, pressing together to seal.

5 Bring a large saucepan of lightly salted water to the boil. Add the ravioli and cook for 15 minutes.

6 Drain the ravioli, using a slotted spoon, and transfer to a large serving dish. Pour over the Italian Red Wine Sauce, sprinkle over the Parmesan cheese and serve immediately.

COOK'S TIP

For square ravioli, divide the dough into two. Wrap half in cling film and thinly roll out the other half. Cover with a clean, damp tea towel while rolling the remaining dough. Spoon the filling at regular intervals and brush the gaps with water or beaten egg. Cover with the second sheet of dough and press firmly between the filling to seal and expel any air. Cut out the shapes with a knife.

Poached Salmon Steaks with Penne

Serves 4

INGREDIENTS

4 x 275 g/10 oz fresh salmon
   steaks
60 g/2 oz/4 tbsp butter
175 ml/6 fl oz/^{3}/4 cup dry
   white wine
sea salt
8 peppercorns
fresh dill sprig
fresh tarragon sprig

1 lemon, sliced
450 g/1 lb dried penne
2 tbsp olive oil
lemon slices and fresh
   watercress, to garnish

LEMON & WATERCRESS
SAUCE:
25 g/1 oz/2 tbsp butter

25 g/1 oz/^{1}/4 cup plain (all
   purpose) flour
150 ml/^{1}/4 pint/^{5}/8 cup warm
   milk
juice and finely grated rind of
   2 lemons
60 g/2 oz watercress, chopped
salt and pepper

1 Put the salmon in a
large, non-stick pan.
Add the butter, wine, a
pinch of sea salt, the
peppercorns, dill, tarragon
and lemon. Cover, bring to
the boil, and simmer for
10 minutes.

2 Using a slotted spoon,
carefully remove the
salmon. Strain and reserve
the cooking liquid.
Remove and discard the
salmon skin and centre

bones. Place on a warm
dish, cover and keep warm.

3 Bring a pan of salted
water to the boil. Add
the penne and 1 tbsp of oil
and cook for 12 minutes.
Drain and sprinkle over the
remaining oil. Place on a
serving dish, top with the
salmon and keep warm.

4 To make the sauce,
melt the butter and stir
in the flour for 2 minutes.

Stir in the milk and about
7 tbsp of the reserved
cooking liquid. Add the
lemon juice and rind and
cook, stirring, for a further
10 minutes.

5 Stir in the watercress
and seasoning.

6 Pour the sauce over
the salmon and penne,
garnish with slices of
lemon and fresh watercress
and serve immediately.

Farfallini Buttered Lobster

Serves 4

INGREDIENTS

2 x 700 g/1 lb 9 oz lobsters,
  split into halves
juice and grated rind of
  1 lemon
115 g/4 oz/^{1}/2 cup butter
4 tbsp fresh white
  breadcrumbs

2 tbsp brandy
5 tbsp double (heavy) cream
  or crème fraîche
450 g/ 1 lb dried farfallini
1 tbsp olive oil
60 g/2 oz/^{2}/3 cup freshly
  grated Parmesan cheese

salt and pepper

TO GARNISH:
1 kiwi fruit, sliced
4 unpeeled, cooked king
  prawns (shrimp)
fresh dill sprigs

1 Carefully discard the stomach sac, vein and gills from each lobster. Remove all the meat from the tail and chop. Crack the claws and legs, remove the meat and chop. Transfer the meat to a bowl and add the lemon juice and rind.

2 Clean the shells thoroughly and place in a warm oven at 170°C/325°/Gas 3 to dry out.

3 Melt 25 g/1 oz/2 tbsp of the butter in a frying pan (skillet). Add the breadcrumbs and fry for about 3 minutes, until crisp and golden brown.

4 Melt the remaining butter in a saucepan and gently cook the lobster meat. Add the brandy and cook for a further 3 minutes, then add the cream or crème fraîche and season to taste.

5 Bring a large pan of lightly salted water to the boil. Add the farfallini and olive oil and cook for about 12 minutes, until tender but still firm to the bite. Drain and spoon the pasta into the clean lobster shells. Top with the buttered lobster and sprinkle with the grated Parmesan cheese and the breadcrumbs. Grill (broil) for 2–3 minutes, until golden brown.

6 Transfer the lobster shells to a warm serving dish, garnish and serve immediately.

Pasta Shells with Mussels

Serves 4–6

INGREDIENTS

1.25 kg/2³/4 lb mussels
225 ml/8 fl oz/1 cup dry white
  wine
2 large onions, chopped
115 g/4 oz/¹/2 cup unsalted
  butter

6 large garlic cloves, finely
  chopped
5 tbsp chopped fresh parsley
300 ml/¹/2 pint/1¹/4 cups
  double (heavy) cream
400 g/14 oz dried pasta shells

1 tbsp olive oil
salt and pepper
crusty bread, to serve

1 Scrub and debeard the mussels under cold running water. Discard any that do not close immediately when tapped. Put the mussels in a pan with the wine and half of the onions. Cover and cook over a medium heat, shaking the pan frequently, until the shells open.

2 Remove from the heat. Drain the mussels and reserve the cooking liquid. Discard any mussels that have not opened. Strain the cooking liquid and reserve.

3 Fry the remaining onion in the butter for 2–3 minutes. Stir in the garlic and cook for 1 minute. Gradually stir in the reserved cooking liquid, parsley and cream. Season and leave to simmer.

4 Cook the pasta with the oil in a pan of salted water until just tender, but still firm to the bite. Drain, return to the pan, cover and keep warm.

5 Reserve a few mussels for the garnish and remove the remainder from their shells. Stir the shelled mussels into the cream sauce and warm briefly. Transfer the pasta to a serving dish. Pour over the sauce and toss well to coat. Garnish with the reserved mussels and serve with warm, crusty bread.

COOK'S TIP

Pasta shells are ideal because the sauce collects in the cavities and impregnates the pasta with flavour.

Baked Scallops with Pasta in Shells

Serves 4

INGREDIENTS

12 scallops	150 ml/^{1}/4 pint/^{5}/8 cup fish	150 ml/^{1}/4 pint/^{5}/8 cup double
3 tbsp olive oil	stock	(heavy) cream
350 g/12 oz/3 cups small,	1 onion, chopped	225 g/8 oz/2 cups grated
dried wholemeal (whole-	juice and finely grated rind of	Cheddar cheese
wheat) pasta shells	2 lemons	salt and pepper
		crusty brown bread, to serve

1 Remove the scallops from their shells. Scrape off the skirt and the black intestinal thread. Reserve the white part (the flesh) and the orange part (the coral or roe). Carefully ease the flesh and coral from the shell with a short, but very strong knife.

2 Wash the shells thoroughly and dry them well. Put the shells on a baking (cookie) sheet, sprinkle lightly with about two thirds of the olive oil and set aside.

3 Meanwhile, bring a large saucepan of lightly salted water to the boil. Add the pasta shells and remaining olive oil and cook for about 12 minutes, until tender, but still firm to the bite. Drain and spoon about 25 g/1 oz of pasta into each scallop shell.

4 Put the scallops, fish stock and onion in an ovenproof dish and season to taste with pepper. Cover with foil and bake in a preheated oven at 180°C/350°F/Gas 4 for 8 minutes.

5 Remove the dish from the oven. Remove the foil and, using a slotted spoon, transfer the scallops to the shells. Add 1 tbsp of the cooking liquid to each shell, drizzle with lemon juice and a little cream, and top with grated cheese.

6 Increase the oven temperature to 230°C/450°F/Gas 8 and return the scallops to the oven for 4 minutes. Serve the scallops in their shells with crusty brown bread and butter.

This is a Parragon Book
First published in 1999
Parragon
Queen Street House
4 Queen Street
Bath BA1 1HE, UK

ISBN: 0-75253-357-6

Copyright © Parragon 1999

All rights reserved. No part of this publication may be reproduced,
stored in a retrieval system or transmitted, in any form or by any means,
electronic, mechanical, photocopying, recording or otherwise, without
the prior permission of the copyright holder.

Printed in China

Note
Cup measurements in this book are for American cups. Tablespoons are
assumed to be 15 ml. Unless otherwise stated, milk is assumed to be
full fat, eggs are medium and pepper is freshly ground black pepper.